— From —
Dry Bones
— to —
Living Hope

Embracing God's Faithfulness in Late Life

Missy Buchanan

UPPER
ROOM BOOKS®
NASHVILLE

Cover design: Emily Weigel
Interior design and typesetting: PerfecType, Nashville, TN

Print ISBN: 978-0-8358-1976-3
Mobi ISBN: 978-0-8358-1977-0
Epub ISBN: 978-0-8358-1978-7

Printed in the United States of America

I dedicate this book to the memory of
Paul Hamm,
a longtime friend whose legacy of humility,
faithfulness, and compassion
shines as a beacon of light to a weary world.

Contents

CONTENTS

Valley of Dry Bones

Ezekiel 37:1-10

The hand of the LORD came upon me, and he brought me out by the Spirit of the LORD and set me down in the middle of a valley; it was full of bones. He led me all around them; there were very many lying in the valley, and they were very dry. He said to me, "Mortal, can these bones live?" I answered, "O Lord GOD, you know." Then he said to me, "Prophesy to these bones, and say to them: O dry bones, hear the word of the LORD. Thus says the Lord GOD to these bones: I will cause breath to enter you, and you shall live. I will lay sinews on you, and will cause flesh to come upon you, and cover you with skin, and put breath in you, and you shall live; and you shall know that I am the LORD."

So I prophesied as I had been commanded; and as I prophesied, suddenly there was a noise, a rattling, and the bones came together, bone to its bone. I looked, and there were sinews on them, and flesh had come upon them, and skin had covered them; but there was no breath in them. Then he said to me, "Prophesy to the breath, prophesy, mortal, and say to the breath: Thus says the Lord GOD: Come from the four winds, O breath, and breathe upon these slain, that they may live." I prophesied as he commanded me, and the breath came into them, and they lived, and stood on their feet, a vast multitude.

LIFE IN THE VALLEY OF DRY BONES

"Prophesy to these bones, and say to them:
O dry bones, hear the word of the LORD."
—EZEKIEL 37:4

There are days when Ezekiel's vision is my
   reality.
A scorched valley stretches out before me as
   far as my eyes can see.
It is a field littered with the remains of once
   vibrant lives.

There is no sign of life—only dry bones. Very
 dry bones.
Everywhere I turn there are worn-out bodies
 like mine.
Frames beaten down by time. Minds bleached
 by the years.
In this season of life, my hope has shriveled
 into nothingness.
How long must I linger in this harsh environ-
 ment, O Lord?
Without purpose and a reason to live, I am
 spiritually dead.
Nothing more than a heap of dry bones.
Then, from the hush of the desert, I hear a
 voice.
Can these bones live?
Lord, you alone know.
Prophesy. Speak to the bones.
So I speak of God's greatness over the ruins.
 The bones begin to rattle and come
 together with sinew and flesh.
But still there is no life.

Prophesy. Speak to the Spirit.

I speak and breath begins to fill the lifeless
bodies.

Breath. Wind. Spirit. The One who hovered
over earth's creation now blows new life
into my declining body.

O Lord, where there is deadness, you bring
new life and hope.

Where there is a dead end, you reveal a way
out of the wilderness.

Come, Holy Spirit, come. Fill me anew, and
let these old bones dance for you once
again!

CULTIVATING HOPE

As we see in Ezekiel's vision, hope does not always
seem possible during dark times. Like your biblical
ancestors in exile, you have known tremendous loss
and grief. You understand what it is like to have relationships, good health, and independence snatched
away as you have grown older. Acknowledging the
hard realities of aging is key to moving forward in

hope. Take your cue from scripture, which is filled with the laments of God's people crying out to God in their grief and suffering. Take comfort in knowing that Jesus modeled lament when he cried out to God in his last hours.

Do not confuse lamenting with complaining or grumbling. Laments are heartfelt prayers that express suffering and loss. They give voice to the deepest cries of your soul. They are also the first step toward moving closer to God on the journey of aging.

- Consider how your life has changed in the last decade. What profound losses have you experienced? Some losses may have come as the result of death. Other losses may have come because of physical changes or unwanted circumstances. Explore your innermost feelings. Then complete this sentence with as many different endings as needed to express your grief and suffering in this season of life:

Gone are the days when _____

_____.

Perhaps your responses are similar to the following:

Gone are the days when *I held my loved one's hand and we laughed together.*

Gone are the days when *I quickly drifted off to sleep and slept through the night.*

Gone are the days when *I drove to special events in the city after dark.*

Gone are the days when *I felt like I had a reason to get up in the morning.*

Say your responses aloud, and then respond with this lament:

O Lord, there have been so many losses in late life. I feel them deep in my dry bones. Come near and comfort me. Hear my cry, O Lord!

■ Ezekiel's vision points you to another important truth that is vital to your journey. Hope is not passive. God called Ezekiel to prophesy over the dry bones. Ezekiel was called to do something. You too are called to take action to move forward in faith. Practice this breath prayer as one way to help you become more conscious of God's presence in your life. When you focus on the miracle of each breath, you will begin to experience something fresh and new. Just as the Holy Spirit filled the lifeless bodies in the Valley of Dry Bones, the Spirit will transform your inner being.

   – *Lord, I am not alone. You are with me in this Valley of Dry Bones.* (Repeat the words, either silently or aloud. Take a deep breath. Hold it for five seconds; then exhale slowly.

   – *Your Spirit empowers me to do what seems impossible.* (Repeat the words, either silently or aloud. Take a deep breath. Hold it for five seconds; then exhale slowly.)

— *Breathe new life into this worn-out body. Fill me with renewed purpose and energy to serve others.* (Repeat the words, either silently or aloud. Take a deep breath. Hold it for five seconds; then exhale slowly.)

BATTLEFIELD

---

*You, O L*ORD*, are a shield around me,*
my glory, and the one who lifts up my head.

—PSALM 3:3

Almost every morning I step onto a battlefield.
From the moment I open my weary eyes,
  I must build up courage to face the
  opposition—
  for the world tells me that aging is my
  enemy.

Culture shouts that I should dread growing
   older. Advertisements incite me to wage
   war using all my resources.
But even anti-aging creams and a healthy lifestyle cannot halt the progression of time.
Each day I try to muster enough courage to
   stare down my fears about late life, but fear
   is a powerful foe that often overtakes me.
Here in the trenches of my mind, I have
   discovered that being alone in my own
   thoughts for too long can be a dangerous
   thing.
From the background noise of the television, I
   hear the enemy mocking me: Young is better than old. Once you get to middle age,
   you are on your way to becoming obsolete.
The message plays over and over in my head
   until I start to believe it.
O Lord, when I feel attacked and vulnerable,
   lift my head and remind me of your truths:
You designed this body to change over time.

You have given me purpose until my final
    breath.
You have assigned me value in old age, even
    when others refuse to acknowledge it.
In the wilderness of aging, a cane and a walker
    are my protection, not a curse or a sign of
    weakness.
Creator God, give me a perspective on aging
    that is shaped by your Word and not by
    the world.
For you have already given me the victory.

CULTIVATING HOPE

Today is a great day to create a new habit of hope-
fulness. Recognize that you are aging in a world
that is obsessed with youth. Commercials and news
pundits assault you with negative thoughts about
aging. One way to confront that reality is to become
more aware of the time you spend watching television or scrolling through social media posts.

- Locate the mute button on your TV remote.
  Every time a commercial comes on, mute the

sound. Use the commercial break to focus instead on scripture. Repeat the following verses during the two- or three-minute break. Be intentional about practicing your new routine until muting the commercials becomes your new habit.

- "Do not be conformed to this world, but be transformed by the renewing of your minds, so that you may discern what is the will of God—what is good and acceptable and perfect" (Rom. 12:2).

- "We do not lose heart. Even though our outer nature is wasting away, our inner nature is being renewed day by day" (2 Cor. 4:16).

- "Let us hold unswervingly to the hope we profess, for he who promised is faithful" (Heb. 10:23, niv).

■ Take this new habit a step forward. Ask yourself some hard questions about your media consumption. While watching news shows or reading posts on social media, do you become agitated or fearful? Do you ever argue with news commentators? Can you sense your heart rate increasing when a friend posts something that directly opposes your opinion?

It is in your best interest to limit your media consumption. You can keep up with the news of the world without drowning yourself in it. Instead of watching hours of news commentary, watch a one-hour news broadcast. Instead of scrolling through social media posts for hours at a time, limit yourself to twenty minutes in the morning and twenty minutes in the afternoon. Be intentional about reducing your exposure to controversy and negative news. Soon you will notice a positive difference in how you feel.

Invisible

"You are the God who sees me."

Genesis 16:13, niv

In this strange land of aging, no one sees me.
I have become invisible, faceless, and nameless
  to strangers who pass me by.
People are too consumed with their own lives
  and smartphones to acknowledge an old
  person like me.
Or maybe they duck their heads and look to
  their feet because they are afraid to really
  see me.

Either way, it is a peculiar thing about growing older.

In waiting rooms and medical offices, staff
members speak to my adult child as if I am
incapable of talking for myself.

Oftentimes people strain to look over me.
Others look around or through me.

It is as though I have somehow been erased
from their line of vision.

Even my own family members ignore me at
times, though not intentionally, I suppose.
Perhaps they believe I have nothing of
value to contribute to a conversation.

I desperately want to cry out, "Can't you see
me? I am right here. Talk to me!"

In a culture so fixated on youth, I feel dis-
missed, ancient, and obsolete.

I yearn for younger people to take me seriously
and not brush me aside just because I do
not know about the latest digital gadget.

O Lord, when the world is swirling around me
but does not include me, my soul shouts, "I
am a child of God!"
Today I will find comfort in knowing that you
are El Roi—*the God who sees me.*

Cultivating Hope

As you have aged in a youth-oriented culture, you
may have felt robbed of your sense of self-worth.
Like many older adults, you wrestle with going
unnoticed and feeling invisible.

It is important to remember that family members can be unintentionally thoughtless. Adult children may think they are helping their aging parent
when they speak on their parent's behalf. They
sometimes fail to understand how they are depriv-
ing their aging parent of dignity and respect. As
the aging parent, you now have an opportunity to
teach them. It is time to give your family members
a gentle reminder that you want to be involved in
discussions about your life and health.

- If you are overlooked in conversations, take the initiative to turn the situation around. Do not wait for others to recognize their oversight. Be brave but grace-filled, and speak up when family members, healthcare officials, or office personnel ignore you. Express your feelings and why you want to be included in conversation.

- Use your life stories as a unique way to let family and friends remember that you still have much to contribute. Scour your cabinets and drawers for small items and photographs that represent meaningful moments from your past. Use these items as storytelling prompts to engage younger listeners. Perhaps it is a patch from your high school letter jacket. Maybe it is a bank ledger that chronicles deposits from your first paying job. It might be an old hand mirror your grandmother gave you on your wedding day. Use the stories to capture the attention of your adult children and grandchildren, then encourage them to ask questions about your life.

For example, tell the younger generations about how you played baseball to earn the letter jacket. Inspire them to work hard for things they want with the bank ledger story about your first job delivering newspapers. Let your grandmother's old hand mirror lead to a funny story about a groomsman whose borrowed suit was five inches too short. Helping others to discover interesting tidbits about your life will give them new perspective and respect.

■ Above all, when you feel invisible to the world, remember the Old Testament story of Hagar, who was banished to the desert. God sought her out in the wilderness and reassured her that she was not forgotten or forsaken. Then God blessed her. Like Hagar, you are never out of God's watchful eye. Reflect on Hagar's story (see Genesis 1:1-16) and what it means to be seen by God as you grow older.

EXILE

I am about to do a new thing;
now it springs forth, do you not perceive it?
I will make a way in the wilderness
and rivers in the desert.

—ISAIAH 43:19

O Lord, it seems I have been cut off from the
world that I have known.
I feel like a captive in a land of despair, cast
away from my homeland and uprooted
from all that is familiar and comforting.

I am an alien—downsized, disoriented, and
   displaced by time and circumstances
   beyond my control.
Here in this strange place, I turn to speak to a
   loved one. But they are not there.
So many friends and family members have
   died over the years.
I am among the last of my generation still
   standing in this wilderness.
Sometimes family members scold me for not
   keeping up with the shifting times, but the
   fast pace of this world unnerves me.
The language of modern culture is foreign to
   me.
Everyday conversations are difficult because I
   struggle with hearing loss.
Feeling incompetent and irrelevant, I close
   myself off.
I become self-exiled in this unsettled time and
   place.
O Lord, liberate me from the prison I've created for myself.

When I feel abandoned, show me someone
 who needs my friendship.
When I want to isolate myself, turn my fear
 into a willingness to try something new.
Change my mindset, God.
Turn this wilderness of dry bones into holy
 ground.
Help me thrive on this journey of aging and
 give you the glory!

Cultivating Hope

You are not alone in your feelings of exile. Like many older adults, you feel displaced as control over your situation diminishes. Perhaps you have been transplanted to a senior community or have moved to another city to be near family. Maybe you are experiencing chronic health issues or going through rehabilitation following surgery. All the while, you are trying to get your bearings in a culture you no longer understand and that does not seem to understand you. Simply put, you feel banished from your familiar homeland. You feel like a wanderer in the wilderness.

It is tempting to hole yourself up in your room until time passes you by. The problem is that God cannot use you if you do not make yourself available. Even in this wilderness experience, God is prompting you to open the door and step out of your comfort zone. God wants you to flourish in this strange land of aging.

- Today, sort through old family photos and study the details carefully. Let the images be reminders of the changes you have experienced in your lifetime. Take note of fashion, hairstyles, and transportation. Consider where you were living and what you were doing in each photo. Then think about how you responded to those life transitions in the past and consider how you felt—uncomfortable? afraid? excited? hopeful? Let the images remind you how change has always been a part of your life. How have changes in the past prepared you to be more resilient now that you are older?

- As appealing as it might be to try to turn back the clock, concentrate on the positive changes that have come with time. What conveniences would you not want to give up at this stage of your life? How has medical technology improved your life or the lives of loved ones? What blessings have you experienced as your family has expanded and changed throughout the years?

- To age well, you must be flexible in your circumstances but steadfast in your faith. Instead of grumbling about the good ol' days, let Isaiah remind you that if you trust God, God will make a way for you through the wilderness.

WHEN PRAISE WILL NOT COME

Why are you cast down, O my soul,
and why are you disquieted within me?

—PSALM 42:5

Almost every day I exercise as I try to keep
   this aging body strong for the journey
   ahead.
Though sometimes I make excuses for not
   walking a mile or riding the stationary
   bike, I try to push through because I know

a sedentary lifestyle is a nemesis of aging
well.

It reminds me of a wooden sign that hangs in
the physical therapy room: *Keep moving.*

But today it is not my body that requires attention; it is my soul.

Outwardly, I am working to keep fit.

Inwardly, I feel sluggish and lazy.

Even through gritted teeth, I cannot summon
enough desire to overcome the malaise and
uselessness that fill my days.

Prayer feels like a lifeless chore, Lord. My pas-
sion has dwindled to a trickle.

I open my mouth to praise you, but the words
stick in my parched throat.

What is wrong with me, Lord? Why is my
soul cast down?

I look around this wasteland of dry bones and
wonder how I can sing a song of praise.

Where is the joy? Where is the laughter?

O God, in this season of drought, let me learn
from the psalmist David, who called his
soul back to you.
Indeed, turning back to you is a means of
moving forward.
Lord, you are mightier than the mixed-up
feelings that churn deep within me.
When life seems an endless struggle, I will
praise you because you alone are sovereign.
When I feel abandoned, I will cry out to you
because you will rescue me.
Today I will reassert my faith in you because
you have always been faithful to me.
I will praise you, one step at a time, as I journey through this wilderness.

Cultivating Hope

The psalmist David understood life in the Valley of
Dry Bones. He knew what it was like to be spiritually thirsty in the wilderness. He felt the mixed-up
emotions that you may be experiencing too.

■ Imagine yourself standing in the sandals of David as you read this passage from Psalm 42:1-6.

As a deer longs for flowing streams,
    so my soul longs for you, O God.
My soul thirsts for God,
    for the living God.
When shall I come and behold
    the face of God?
My tears have been my food
    day and night,
while people say to me continually,
    "Where is your God?"

These things I remember,
    as I pour out my soul:
how I went with the throng,
    and led them in procession to the
        house of God,
with glad shouts and songs of
        thanksgiving,
    a multitude keeping festival.

Why are you cast down, O my soul,
  and why are you disquieted within
    me?
Hope in God; for I shall again praise
  him,
    my help and my God.

On the journey of aging, you have shared David's feelings. You too have been spiritually dry and thirsty. You have cried pools of tears over losses. Like David, you have felt the inner struggle of voices competing in your head. What then can you learn from David's wilderness experience?

The scripture affirms that David talked to himself to call his own soul back to God. He went back in his memory to remember how he worshiped previously to avow how he would worship again. Follow David's lead back to God. Recall moments in your past when you felt especially close to God. Remember times when you sang hymns with great gusto or felt God's presence beside you during prayer.

Return to those moments in your mind and let them usher in hope.

- You may also need to change your habits to feed your soul. Do not wait for a Sunday morning worship service to get in a worshipful mood. Find favorite hymns or praise music on your digital device, or ask a family member to bring you a CD player and CD of worship music so you can play it during the week. Let the music of worship become the background to your day. Invite the words to seep into your soul. Sing with the recordings. Listen to them over and over. Let your heart be strengthened by worshipful music and feel your spirits lift throughout the day.

TEMPTATIONS IN THE WILDERNESS

God is faithful; he will not let you be tempted
beyond what you can bear.
—1 CORINTHIANS 10:13, NIV

I am a vagabond in this rugged land of aging.
Without a career or a family to raise in this
    season of life, I drift aimlessly through my
    days without direction or focus.
My independence is gradually slipping away,
    and I am forced to rely on the help of

others to do mundane tasks I once could
do myself.

In my frustration at losing control, I sometimes
become a person I never wanted to be.

Suddenly I am the stereotype of an older adult:
a grumbler, a complainer, a curmudgeon.

O Lord, why do I give in to the temptations of
aging?

When I get up in the morning, I do not intend
to be cranky.

But by midday, I am already out of sorts with
a newcomer who sits in my seat in the dining room.

I become impatient with the hard-working
housekeeper who rearranged my belongings on the counter.

I spew a thoughtless comment about a young
person's tattoo.

How did I become a critical spirit, so unwill-
ing to embrace change in this season of
late life?

Why do I wallow in my self-centered woes,
    whining and moaning so much that I drive
    others away?
O Lord, I confess my sinfulness. I do not want
    to be known for selfish and prideful ways.
Give me grace to be less prickly and more pli-
    able as I grow older.
Reorient my thoughts toward you, O God.
    Exchange my judgmental attitude for joy
    in this great adventure of life.
Let your Spirit close my lips when I am about
    to say something that is hurtful or selfish.
Help me be the person you want me to be.

CULTIVATING HOPE

Resisting temptation does not get easier as you grow older. In fact, it takes a big dose of humility to admit your vulnerability to sinfulness in later years. The good news is that you can turn your temptations into opportunities to model faithful aging for younger generations.

Review this list of common temptations, and identify those that present the greatest challenge for you.

1. Critical spirit: Do you often criticize others?
2. Spiritually retired: Do you believe that at this stage of life you have earned the right to put your feet up and not pursue spiritual growth and service opportunities?
3. Inflexible: Do you resist and complain about the changes in your life?
4. Self-pity: Do you spend time feeling sorry for yourself?
5. Worry: Are you consumed with the "what ifs" in your future?
6. Regret: Are you filled with guilt, shame, or remorse about the past?

As you consider where you feel tempted in your life, invite God's Spirit to speak to you through this passage: "No temptation has overtaken you except what is common to mankind. And God is faithful; he will not let you be tempted beyond what you can bear. But when you are tempted, he will also provide a way out so that you can endure it" (1 Cor. 10:13, NIV). Pay close attention to the last sentence of this passage. You can be confident that God will provide a way for you to endure the temptations that come with aging.

- One way to deal with the temptations of aging is to practice substituting a positive response for a negative one. Instead of criticizing the person who sits in your seat in the dining room, compliment them on their nice smile. Instead of grumbling about a young adult's tattoo, lead with curiosity. Ask them to share the significance or meaning of the design, and listen without making a negative comment.

    There may be times you are not even aware of your own negativity. Enlist the aid of a trusted, spiritually mature friend to help you see beyond your own blind spots and hold you accountable. Invite that friend to use a code phrase if you start to grumble in their presence. For example, invite them to softly say,

"Grace, my friend" as a gentle reminder that you are yielding to your critical spirit. With humility and practice, you will learn to catch yourself before you start to criticize others.

- If you are tempted to sink into your recliner and spend the entire afternoon watching reruns on television, shift your mindset away from yourself. Get up and do something to encourage another person. Write a letter to a grandchild. Call an old friend who is in rehab. Contact a friend who recently lost their spouse. Look beyond yourself for opportunities to serve others.

- If your greatest temptation is being a constant worrier, take positive action to counteract your anxiety. When worrisome "what ifs" fill your mind, redirect your thoughts to Jesus' words from the Gospel of John. Repeat them until you have them memorized. "Peace I leave with you; my peace I give to you. I do not give to you as the world gives. Do not let your hearts be troubled, and do not let them be afraid" (John 14:27).

From Wasteland to Wildflowers

The desert and the parched land will be glad;
the wilderness will rejoice and blossom.
—ISAIAH 35:1, NIV

Today the spiritual desert of aging seems
    uninspiring and boring.
Like my daily routine, the wilderness land-
    scape feels monotonous and drab.
I take the same route. I eat the same food. I
    watch the same shows.

Then I do it all over again until Monday
blurs into Tuesday, and Tuesday blurs into
Wednesday.
O God, my days are as lifeless and dry as the
desert.
Where is the beauty of late life? Where is the
joy?
In the distance, desert winds begin to stir.
Dark clouds blow across the vast sky, bringing a soaking rain and hope to this thirsty
soul.
Soon the seeds that have lain dormant for so
long explode with vibrant color.
The landscape that was dry and lifeless is now
awash in wildflowers.
My eyes can barely take in the splendor. How
can anything so magnificent take root in
this hostile land?
Lord, you alone bring forth the miracle of
transformation.

Desert plants are resilient. They have adapted
to their environment, and they flourish
under your watchful care.

Like the wildflowers, I want to joyfully adapt
to my environment.

Let me age in your undefeatable hope.

Use me to bring unexpected delight to those
around me who are weary of life in the
Valley of Dry Bones.

Amid monotony, let me be a colorful, living testimony to your steadfast love and
faithfulness.

CULTIVATING HOPE

You may be experiencing a season of life that feels
like the desert wilderness. Life has become so routine that it feels uninteresting and uninspiring.
Sometimes you begin to question if God has forgotten you. Throughout the Bible, God uses the desert
experience to shape people for God's purposes.

Changing your environment may be impossible. There are certain physical limitations you

may be forced to endure. Whatever your situation, God is calling you to adapt joyfully like the desert wildflowers. Instead of woefully trudging through the day, God wants to help you see that this season is ripe with opportunities to reveal God's glory to those around you. When you accept the things that you cannot change, you will soon discover surprising possibilities all around you.

- Picture the stunning beauty of the wildflowers set against the barren landscape. Read this passage from Isaiah, and use the mental image as inspiration to create moments of unexpected joy for others.

The desert and the parched land will
    be glad;
  the wilderness will rejoice and
    blossom.
Like the crocus, it will burst into
    bloom;
  it will rejoice greatly and shout for
    joy.

The glory of Lebanon will be given
    to it,
  the splendor of Carmel and
    Sharon;
they will see the glory of the Lord,
  the splendor of our God.

Strengthen the feeble hands,
  steady the knees that give way;
say to those with fearful hearts,
  "Be strong, do not fear;
your God will come,
  he will come with vengeance;
  with divine retribution
    he will come to save you."
    (Isa. 35:1-4, niv)

Think of things you can do to put a smile on the face of at least five people. Give a book with a handwritten note to a neighbor. Find a funny joke, and share it with others during lunch. Slide a copy of an uplifting devotion under the doorway of someone who is feeling depressed. In ways big and small, you are called to reflect God's glory. Use your life in the wilderness to lift others' spirits.

- Perhaps it is time to disrupt your own routine. Be intentional about breaking the monotony of your late life. Today take a different route. Try a new food you have never tasted before. Watch a documentary instead of your favorite cable news show. In small ways, practice being flexible throughout your day. Joy will come as you escape the dryness of too much routine.

DIGITAL DIVIDE

Let the wise listen and add to their learning.
—PROVERBS 1:5, NIV

The journey of aging has taken me to a look-
out known as the Digital Divide.
The path to get to here was rocky and uneven,
causing me to stumble on unfamiliar
things like passwords, apps, and virtual
meetings.
Now as I scan the scene before me, I realize
that the Digital Divide is a deep canyon

FROM DRY BONES TO LIVING HOPE

separating people by age and knowledge of
technology.
On the side where I stand are others like me
who are intimidated by electronic devices.
We are older people who become anxious
when trying to remember the instructions
for using social media and video chatting.
Across the divide are younger people who
were born knowing how to navigate digital
tools at lightning speed. They are fearless,
and they sometimes mock us older learners
because we are slow and cautious.
The gap between our two sides seems to widen
as the pace of technology speeds up.
So here we are facing one another, yet two
worlds apart. Young and old.
There are days when I wonder if I will ever be
able to learn enough about technology to
help bridge the great divide.
O God, I fear I am too old to learn so many
new things. I am afraid I am incapable of
keeping up.

What if I make a mistake and damage my
device? What if I fall prey to a scam or a
computer virus?
Lord, give me confidence to try and try again
when I feel incompetent.
Show me how to be brave in this strange land
of the Digital Divide.

Cultivating Hope

As you have journeyed from one season of life to
the next, you may have discovered that the route
takes you through the wilderness. Think back to
your first job interview. Most likely you felt an overwhelming sense of insecurity and fear. Now you
are once again having a wilderness experience. This
time though, the wilderness has a name: *technology*.

When asked to name things that cause them
anxiety, most older adults put digital technology
near the top of their list. Just trying to learn the
unfamiliar vocabulary associated with computers,
the Internet, and smartphones is enough to make
you break out in a sweat. But in truth, mastering

basic technology skills is key for you to connect with family and friends, both near and far. Technology also offers you infinite learning opportunities without ever leaving your living room.

- Take a moment to reflect on those times in your life when you were afraid to try something new, but you did it anyway because of the great potential it held. Maybe it was leaving for college as a young adult. Perhaps it was giving birth to a first child. In these situations, the excitement and anticipation of something wonderful overruled your fear. Now it is time to gather your courage again and look to a positive outcome. You can do this!

- Confront the plethora of excuses you have imagined for not learning to use technology. It is true you must be cautious of scams and viruses. It is also a reality that your digital device may falter from time to time. However, do not lose sight of the positive opportunities that technology can bring to your life.

Take the risk. Sign up for the computer class. Ask a grandchild to assist you with social media. You are smarter than you think. You can still learn new things. Change the trajectory of your life by embracing your fears. Stay teachable as you age.

- To believe that you have learned all you need to know is a perilous temptation of aging. Be brave and open your mind to learning something new. Read this passage from Proverbs and let the words soak into your dry bones: "Let the wise listen and add to their learning, and let the discerning get guidance" (1:5, NIV).

Remembering

Memory is a peculiar thing. Most days, I can't
    recall what I had for lunch.
Or I stare blankly into the face of someone
    familiar because their name has escaped me.
O Lord, forgetting things is both embarrass-
    ing and terrifying.
When my memory falters, I am inclined to
    panic. I begin to think that dementia has

crept in like a deadly vulture waiting to
devour me in this wilderness of aging.

I start to wonder who I would be without my
memories.

On most afternoons I try to stimulate my
mind with word puzzles stacked beside my
easy chair.

I watch game shows and celebrate the rare
moments when I beat a contestant to the
right answer.

Occasionally I even surprise myself by recit-
ing every word to a poem or Bible verse I
learned as a child.

With each passing day, I work more intentionally to remember so that I do not forget.

O God, I confess that I have tried harder to
remember names and faces and facts from
my past than I have to remember you.

You have never forgotten me, Lord. You still
call me by name.

On this journey of aging, my faithfulness to
you has sometimes dissolved into half-
hearted acts of worship.
I gripe and forget that you parted the Red Sea.
I convince myself that I have no purpose and
forget how mightily you used Moses and
Abraham in their late years.
I turn a blind eye to the cross and forget that
you have promised me salvation.
Lord, forgive me for not intentionally remembering you.
Here in the Valley of Dry Bones, awaken my
memories of you, O God.
Stir up my recollections of your strength and
power.
Help me remember . . . help me to remember
you.

Cultivating Hope

God knows that God's people are always in dan-
ger of losing their spiritual memory. By Monday
morning, you can't recall the message of Sunday's

sermon. You moan about the food at breakfast and glance at a stunning sunset without giving thanks to the One who created it. It is as though you must relearn what it is to be a faithful follower each day. Perhaps that is why remembering is a dominant theme of the Bible.

The story of Joshua is just one example of the importance of remembering that is captured in scripture.

> Joshua summoned the twelve men from the Israelites, whom he had appointed, one from each tribe. Joshua said to them, "Pass on before the ark of the LORD your God into the middle of the Jordan, and each of you take up a stone on his shoulder, one for each of the tribes of the Israelites, so that this may be a sign among you. When your children ask in time to come, 'What do those stones mean to you?' then you shall tell them that the waters of the Jordan were cut off in front of the ark of the covenant of the LORD. When it crossed over the

Jordan, the waters of the Jordan were cut off. So these stones shall be to the Israelites a memorial forever." (Josh. 4:4-7)

The stacked stones were meant to be a visual reminder to God's people to stop and remember what God had done in their lives. The scripture also reveals that remembering is not intended just for ourselves; it is for future generations too.

- Like the stones that were a signal to remember God, you have an object that could become a reminder of God's faithfulness in your life. Look around. Maybe it is something from nature or a special photograph of the mountains or beach. Perhaps it is a small cross or a rock painted by a grandchild. Whatever the item, move it to a new place where you will notice it each day. Put it on your bathroom counter. Hang it on a door handle. Place it beside your remote control. Whenever you see the object, let it signal you to remember God's goodness in your life.

- Another way to exercise your spiritual memory is to complete this sentence in as many ways as you can. Repeat it daily and continue to add new endings as you reflect and remember.

By God's power and faithfulness, I _____

_____.

Use these examples as inspiration to create your own responses:

By God's power and faithfulness, I *survived a bout with cancer.*

By God's power and faithfulness, I *found joy in the midst of deep grief for my beloved spouse.*

By God's power and faithfulness, I *successfully raised my children as a single parent.*

Becoming more mindful of God's movement in your past is key to aging faithfully and noticing God's presence in the here and now. Whenever you sing hymns, reflect on the lyrics and remember

God. Listen attentively to a sermon or study the scriptures and be reminded of the unshakable promises of God. Be intentional about creating a practice to remember God's faithfulness so that you do not forget.

GRIEF BEFORE DEATH

---

*Be merciful to me, L*ORD*, for I am in distress;*
my eyes grow weak with sorrow,
my soul and body with grief.
—PSALM 31:9, NIV

Lately I have been wondering: Is it possible
    to grieve the loss of someone even though
    they have not died?
I am learning that grief does not always begin
    at a graveside; sometimes it starts with a
    diagnosis or a frantic phone call.

FROM DRY BONES TO LIVING HOPE

I have also found that grief rushes in when
    I finally admit harsh realities that I have
    been desperately trying to deny—
I am no longer a safe driver.
My loved one is showing signs of dementia.
I need help to care for myself and my home.
Little by little I am coming to grips with the
    fact that life will never go back to how it
    once was.
O Lord, the losses of late life are piling up like
    dry bones in the desert.
This heartache is not only about the decline or
    death of people I love.
I also am heavy with sorrow over my loss of
    independence and the unmet dreams I had
    for the future.
Here in this harsh land, my grief is exhausting
    and lonely.
There are no support groups for mourning the
    loss of a home and belongings.

There is no self-help book for overcoming the
disappointment of not being able to drive
myself wherever I want to go.

O God, this mourning is real but so is your
love.

Beneath the debris and ash of loss, your Spirit
moves.

This season of grief is a doorway to hope.

You who brought life back to dry bones will
bring new life to me.

Cultivating Hope

Sometimes you feel as though death is pounding
at your door. Your days are crammed with funerals
and medical appointments—grim reminders that
you cannot escape loss and death in late years. Here
in the Valley of Dry Bones, life often feels bleak.

As an older adult, you have a frame of refer-
ence for grief and loss that is different from that of
your younger counterparts. Aside from mourning
the death of friends and family, you also are grieving the person you once were. You feel the loss of

identity that came from your career and the roles that shaped who you are. Without these labels, you may feel as though you don't know who you are anymore. At the same time, you are experiencing the loss of independence, health, home, and belongings.

- Take time today to sit with your feelings of loss. Let your mind explore things you are mourning in this season of life. As with laments, it is important to acknowledge those losses. Be honest. Whatever you are grieving, God invites you to pour out your feelings before God. Let the words of this psalm lead the way:

  Trust in him at all times, O people;
  pour out your heart before him;
  God is a refuge for us. (Ps. 62:8)

- Part of your role as a faithful elder is to help younger generations better understand grief and loss in old age so they can learn to respond with compassion and understanding. You may feel that they trivialize your pain when they say things like, "He's in a better place" as you grieve the loss of a spouse or friend. Or maybe it seems they are glossing over your feelings when they downplay the emotional toll of leaving your beloved home to move to a senior living community. With words of grace, you have an opportunity to teach them about loss and aging.

If reminiscing about your deceased loved one brings you comfort, explain to your family that you enjoy hearing them share their memories. On days when you are weary of being alone, be courageous enough to ask them to join you for dinner. Friends and family will be relieved to know of ways they can support you. Share your experiences of grief as one way to help younger generations better prepare for their own journey of aging.

Vulnerable in the Valley

---

*Do you not know that your body is a temple
of the Holy Spirit within you, which you have
from God, and that you are not your own?*
—1 Corinthians 6:19

For most of my life, I have considered myself
 a tough, self-made individual in control of
 my own destiny.
Now I am not so sure.
Here in the wilderness of aging, all pretense
 is stripped away, and I realize how truly
 mortal I am.

This time-swept landscape offers no place to
hide. O Lord, in this wilderness I cannot
pretend that I can do it all alone, no matter
how hard I try.
My vulnerability as an aging mortal is
fully exposed—physically, emotionally,
spiritually.
As I look back over my long life, I confess that
my idea of success and independence was
often driven by egotistical pride. There
were many times I gave myself credit that
was due you, God.
Here in the Valley of Dry Bones, I recognize
now how desperately I need you.
I feel so vulnerable.
I worry that one day I will become a burden
on my family.
Daily I am reminded that I am at-risk for fall-
ing, chronic disease, and loneliness.
With the soaring costs of health care and care-
giving, I am concerned that my money
may not be enough to last my lifetime.

O Lord, just as life seems so bleak and bare, I
look up to see a sunrise cresting the horizon of this vast wilderness.
Every morning without fail, you bring a sign
of hope and set the sky ablaze in your
faithfulness.
On this journey of aging, I am learning that
I must be willing to ask for help from
friends and family, knowing that you, O
Lord, send my loved ones to my aid.
Though I am vulnerable, you are always a
promise keeper. There is my hope.

Cultivating Hope

As your body changes over time so does your perspective on mortality. When you were younger, you
felt invincible. You were strong and self-assured, and
you rarely gave thought to the fragility and imper-
manence of earthly life. But along the way something happened. A loved one was diagnosed with a
life-threatening illness. A dear friend was killed in
a car accident. Or maybe you experienced an event

that shook your sense of self-reliance and control to the core: an unexpected job loss, bankruptcy, or an unwanted divorce. In the aftershock, you quickly discovered that invincibility is just an illusion.

- Recall a time recently when you felt physically vulnerable. Perhaps you took a tumble when you tripped on a rug. Maybe you huffed and puffed your way up a single flight of stairs. Think about the emotions you experienced when you had to admit to yourself that your strength and agility are waning.

- Certainly, the journey of aging ushers you toward an acceptance of your own mortality. However, even though losing physical stamina and abilities in late life is common, there are ways to minimize the effects. Since unexpected falls can cause serious injuries, be proactive. Ask your church, senior living community, or healthcare provider to host a fall-prevention class for older adults. Certified trainers or physical therapists will demonstrate how you can prevent many falls through improved balance and strength exercises. They will also suggest practical safety modifications to your home and will address additional reasons that many older adults fall, including medications and vision issues.

- Remember that God did not design the human body to last forever. You have important choices to make even though you have limited control over how your body will age. Let First Corinthians be your guide. Read this passage often as you seek to glorify God by caring for your body:

> Do you not know that your body is a temple of the Holy Spirit within you, which you have from God, and that you are not your own? For you were bought with a price; therefore glorify God in your body. (1 Cor. 6:19-20)

- Reject the idea that your worn-out body no longer needs care and attention. Learn to love your physical body as tenderly as a vintage-car collector cares for a classic automobile. Even with some corrosion over time, your body is still God's holy design, and God intends for you to care for it as best you can.

Though you are tempted to spend hour after hour in your favorite recliner, being a good steward of your aging body requires that you get moving. Take advantage of exercise programs in your community. Take a brisk walk for thirty minutes a day, if possible. Participate in chair aerobics, or stretch your muscles through chair yoga. Look for fitness programs on television or online that inspire you. Find an exercise regimen that works for you and stick with it. Exercise will not turn back time, but you will glorify God as you become a good steward of your aging body.

The Path to Purpose

Even to old age and gray hairs,
O God, do not forsake me,
until I proclaim your might
to all the generations to come.

—PSALM 71:18

I am surrounded by older people just waiting
to die.
They go through the motions of living, but in
truth, a part of their spirit is wasting away.

Their sense of purpose has withered like the
dry bones. On most days they sit in tight
circles and grumble or gossip.

O Lord, I am terrified of becoming one of
them.

Here in the wilderness of old age, I have seen
how depression and pain can dry up life-
giving purpose.

It vanishes like a trickle of water that seeps
into a parched riverbed and disappears into
the sunbaked desert floor.

I ache for the Spirit to bring renewed purpose
to my life.

But what is the purpose of coming alive if no
one is interested in who I am or what I
have to say?

What is the purpose of having a revitalized
inner life if I am still slow and unable to
keep up with younger generations?

O God, what is my divine purpose in old age?

What can I contribute at this stage of my life?

Without purpose, I feel hope draining away
from this aging body.
Today I will fix my eyes on you, Lord. When
I begin to question my purpose, I will
remember that you created me to love you,
to know you more, and to reflect your
glory to others.
May your divine purpose guide my steps.

Cultivating Hope

What is the point of growing old? You may feel as though aging has robbed you of the ability to contribute to the world in a meaningful way. What reason could God have for keeping you around in this season of life?

You are not alone in your struggle. This question—*What is my purpose, God?*—is one that continues to puzzle and frustrate older Christians around the globe. What is your purpose now that you have no career? What is your purpose now that you cannot drive? What is your purpose now that your family is raised and scattered among different time zones? In truth, you would prefer a detailed job description with bullet points to explain precisely what God is calling you to do in this season of life. You would like for God to spell out your specific Christian responsibilities in old age because your purpose seems a mystery.

Even when you feel tempted to question God's wisdom for leaving you on the earth for so long, especially if you have chronic health issues or are experiencing loss, remind yourself that as one of God's senior saints, you have been given a special assignment.

So what is your special assignment? Who does God want you to influence with your late years? How can you use your gifts and talents in different ways than ever before? In late life, you are called to be a witness to God's grace and faithfulness. You have lived many years and have accumulated an array of life experiences in which God revealed God's self in mighty ways. Your divine purpose in this current season involves using your experiences to bless others by sharing your testimony of God's grace in your life. How will you complete your special assignment?

- Consider that part of your divine purpose is to teach younger people how to grow old faithfully. Never forget that others are watching and learning about aging from you even when you are not aware. Caregivers, friends, family, strangers—they are all learning by observing you. Seize the moment and teach them well.
- The story of Anna, an eighty-four-year-old prophet, can be found in the Gospel of Luke. Though Anna's narrative is short, it reveals a long-reaching witness. Be inspired by the words of scripture.

> There was also a prophet, Anna the daughter of Phanuel, of the tribe of Asher. She was of a great age, having lived with her husband seven years after her marriage, then as a widow to the age of eighty-four. She never left the temple but worshiped there

with fasting and prayer night and day. At that moment she came, and began to praise God and to speak about the child to all who were looking for the redemption of Jerusalem. (Luke 2:36-38)

Notice that Anna did not allow her late age to become an excuse just to nap on the sofa. She continued to praise the Lord through prayer and fasting until the very end of her life. Today, reflect on how you too can use your life to worship God more fervently. Think bigger than Sunday morning worship. It is part of your divine purpose!

Forgiveness

I can do all things through him who
strengthens me.
—PHILIPPIANS 4:13

Here in the wilderness I spend a lot of time
   wandering around the past in my mind.
Wounds from long ago fester, seeping anger
   and bitterness into my old bones—a
   betrayal, a rejection, a life-shattering lie.
I thought I had moved past the unforgettable
   injustice that caused me such pain. But I
   have not.

At my age, why do I feel such resentment,
  Lord?
Why can't I let old transgressions scatter like
  chaff in the wind?
Standing in the rubble of broken relationships,
  I realize that it is far easier to talk about
  forgiving someone than to actually do it.
Even after all these years, I long to hear the
  words *I'm sorry*, but I doubt I ever will.
Forgiveness without an apology seems such an
  impossible task, O Lord. It feels like put-
  ting a gold star on their bad behavior.
Still, I yearn for the brokenness in my life to
  be restored before it is too late.
It is difficult to admit, but I must also accept
  my own role in relationships gone wrong.
How many times have you forgiven me for my
  own shortcomings and failures, God?
Redeem the pain that aches in this repentant
  heart.
Even if there is no reconciliation, forgiveness
  will make my journey easier.

In this late season of life, I need to forgive
others. I need to forgive myself.
To forgive is to live.

CULTIVATING HOPE

Scanning the horizon of the vast wilderness is
much like reviewing the span of your long life. You
can see the accumulation of your life experiences,
both good and bad, spread out before you. You can
pinpoint moments when someone broke their trust
with you. Though you have tried to forgive them,
the wounds have never healed.

To age faithfully requires that you practice forgiveness in response to God's forgiveness of you.
However, you know from experience that talking about forgiveness in the abstract is far easier
than doing it. How do you forgive an abusive
family member? How do you deal with the emotions that remain after a parent abandoned you or
a spouse broke their vow? Certainly, some behaviors feel harder to forgive than others. Acknowledge the reality of what happened, the pain that

it caused, and how it affected your life. Revisiting these wounds can be painful, and you may want to speak with a trusted friend, family member, or pastor about your feelings. Once you have taken time to grieve, ask the Spirit to lead you out of the wilderness of unforgiveness.

- Forgiveness is not about affirming past bad behavior. It is about letting go of negative emotions that are causing you perpetual angst in late life. Forgiveness is crucial to living your last years in peace. Read this passage from the Gospel of Matthew that begins the parable of the unmerciful servant:

  > Peter came and said to him, "Lord, if another member of the church sins against me, how often should I forgive? As many as seven times?" Jesus said to him, "Not seven times, but, I tell you, seventy-seven times." (Matt. 18:21-22)

Take note that Jesus teaches us that true forgiveness is not a one-and-done deal but a process. Forgiveness is a series of decisions that you make over a period of time. Reflect on that important truth. Then ask God for the power to help you move toward the goal of forgiveness.

- Over time, you have learned that the burden of unforgiveness is heavy. Carrying around anger and bitterness is detrimental to your health and well-being. Maybe the person who offended you is no longer alive, but the pain still seethes within you. Or perhaps you are struggling with the guilt of a wrong you did to someone else. Take a step in releasing these burdens to God. Name three people you need to forgive. Then name three things for which you would like to be forgiven.

- When you feel a rush of negative emotions about a past wrong deed, pause and take a breath. Think about the Bible's greatest example of forgiveness. Jesus was betrayed, falsely accused, beaten, and unjustly put to death. Yet from the cross, Jesus cried out, "Father, forgive them; for they do not know what they are doing" (Luke 23:34). Even when forgiveness is hard, let Jesus' example show you the way.

Persistently Patient

Be patient, beloved,
until the coming of the Lord.

—James 5:7

Life in the wilderness is a time of waiting.
I wait for family and friends to visit and for
    the pastor to knock on my door.
I wait for the doctor to call with test results
    and for prescriptions to be filled.
I wait for the mail to arrive and for people to
    get off their smartphones.

I wait for banana pudding on Wednesday
evenings and for card games on Friday
afternoons.

In the hush of the midnight hours, I wait and
wonder who will be next. Who in my circle
of friends and family will be the next to die?

It is like a deeply guarded secret that everyone
knows but no one dares to utter aloud.

The reality is that we are all elders-in-waiting.

Some people say the wilderness of aging is
God's waiting room, a place where I am
destined to do mindless arts and crafts
until my name is called.

Lord, I am confident that you intend for late
life to be more than waiting for the final
roll call.

So I wonder—*Am I wasting my late years waiting to die, or am I using these years to fulfill
your calling?*

God, I have discovered that waiting is not
passive. Nor is it about keeping my hands
busy while the hours tick by.

You are showing me that waiting faithfully can
lead to transformation. It is about growing
more Christlike with each passing day.
Lord, help me to be persistently patient as I
grow older.
Teach me to wait with purpose, knowing that
you are using each experience to better
prepare me to return to you one day.
Help me use the gift of time to encourage others and draw closer to you.
Even as I wait in the wilderness, you never
make me wait alone.

Cultivating Hope

Scripture tells you to wait on the Lord, but you live
in an impatient world that demands instant grati-
fication. God is calling you to model faithful, persistent patience. Reflect on God's counsel in the
psalmist's words, and consider how you are using
time in this season of late life: "Wait for the Lord;
be strong, and let your heart take courage; wait for
the Lord!" (Ps. 27:14).

- Think about different ways you experience time on the journey of aging. When does time seem to go quickly? In what ways does time seem to move slowly? Ponder the different emotions you have recently experienced while waiting. For example, if a grandchild were coming to visit, you may have experienced waiting as a time of excitement and anticipation. If you were standing in a long line at the store, you likely felt frustrated or weary. When you waited by the phone for the news of a loved one's medical crisis, you probably felt unsettled and anxious. When has waiting been especially difficult for you in the last few weeks? What made it difficult? What was your response?

- Like many older adults, you may find practicing patience to be challenging on days when your body is aching from arthritis or another chronic health issue. In the book of Romans, Paul offers three short directives that will help you on the journey of aging: "Rejoice in hope, be patient in suffering, persevere in prayer" (Rom. 12:12). How has your health impacted your patience? What can you learn from Paul's three directives that will help you wait faithfully in response to what God has done for you through Jesus?

- If you are like many older adults, you silently ponder the timing of your own death. With each birthday that rolls around, you wonder if it will be your last. Maybe you feel like you are biding time in a waiting room just outside death's door. Remember, God is more interested in how you are using your late life than in the date on your death certificate. How are you actively pursuing growth as a disciple of Jesus? In what specific ways are you seeking a deeper relationship with God? How do you need to show more restraint and patience as you age?

COMMUNITY

Let us consider how we may spur one another
on toward love and good deeds, not giving
up meeting together, as some are in the habit
of doing, but encouraging one another.
—HEBREWS 10:24-25, NIV

The Valley of Dry Bones can be a solitary
place.
Friends die or move away. Family members get
busy with their own lives.
Some days I feel the despair of isolation deep
within my bones.

I look around the barren landscape and yearn
   for others to come alongside me.
Lord, I need faithful friends to encourage me
   when the wilderness experience becomes
   grueling.
I long for compassionate friends to sit with me
   when I mourn.
I need wise companions to hold me account-
   able when I become too critical.
And I believe they need me too.
O God, in the Valley of Dry Bones, the dust
   of death fills my nostrils.
I am desperate for life-giving relationships
   that take me beyond myself.
Give me opportunities to bask in the conta-
   gious laughter of children and youth.
Let me experience companionship with young
   families and empty-nesters.
For none of us can flourish alone.
Old and young, we need one another, and we
   need you, Lord.

Some of us are weary and worn; others are
   energetic but frenzied by the world's
   expectations.
O God, send your Spirit to breathe new life
   into all generations.
Fill us with compassion and humility so that
   we can affirm and learn from one another.
Together we will reclaim the joy of intergenerational relationships that will turn this
   wilderness experience into a glimpse of
   heaven.
Rise up, bones of all generations!

Cultivating Hope

The wilderness experience of aging can be lonely
without the support and encouragement of others.
In fact, staying connected to family and friends and
to a faith community is vital to your well-being on
the journey of aging. Yet maintaining those con-
nections may become more difficult as time passes.

   Perhaps you have already outlived close companions who were a source of spiritual strength

and encouragement for you. Or maybe you have moved to a new place, leaving longtime relationships behind. Now you feel like the dry bones in Ezekiel's vision—disconnected and disjointed.

- The importance of having a strong, supportive faith community as you grow older cannot be overstated. Take an account of your current situation. Are you trying to navigate life without a faith community at your side? How has your faith community changed over the last few years? With whom do you regularly experience spiritual support and meaningful fellowship? Do you have younger friends who are encouragers?

- Study this passage from Hebrews and consider its significance for your late life:

    Let us hold unswervingly to the hope
    we profess, for he who promised is
    faithful. And let us consider how
    we may spur one another on toward
    love and good deeds, not giving up

meeting together, as some are in the habit of doing, but encouraging one another—and all the more as you see the Day approaching. (Heb. 10:23-25, NIV)

Notice that the writer of Hebrews emphasizes the importance of meeting together and encouraging one another. It is easy to unintentionally drift away from a community of believers as you undergo changes that come with aging, but the need for community remains vital—regardless of age.

If you are not already part of a small group or a Bible study, perhaps God is calling you to organize a community of faith partners who will pray for and encourage one another on the journey of aging. Take inspiration from the scripture. Reach out to the staff of your senior community or your church's pastoral staff to assist you in creating a small group that meets weekly. Ask them to help you find appropriate study materials and to provide leadership as needed.

- Growing older in faith is also an intergenerational affair. As an older adult, you have both an opportunity and an obligation to nurture relationships with younger generations. Reflect on this verse from Psalm 145: "One generation commends your works to another; they tell of your mighty acts" (v. 4, NIV).

Notice that each generation tells of God's work to another generation, and this does not mean that only older generations can teach or minister to young generations. Younger people have stories to share with older generations too. To encourage their participation, you must be willing to listen without judgment. Take responsibility for creating opportunities to share common interests with younger generations. Then use these moments as springboards for conversation about your faith journeys.

One idea is to read books that are on the required reading list for upper elementary, middle school, or high school students. Offer to participate in a book discussion with the students as part of a youth ministry event. Or create your own conversation with a grand-child around a book that you select together. Be attentive to the thoughts of the young people. Ask them to share their opinions. Be prepared to share your thoughts too. Let the book exercise be a stepping-stone to sharing faith stories.

- Another way to set the foundation for sharing stories of faith is to intentionally make yourself vulnerable to younger people. Tell them about the times you were bullied as a young person. Recall situations when you failed at something. Share with them the heartache you felt when you were not invited to a special event. Disclosing feelings of insecurity has a way of bringing generations together.

Allow your vulnerability to lead to deeper relationships.

Divine Interruptions

I heard the voice of the Lord saying,
"Whom shall I send? And who will go for us?"
And I said, "Here am I. Send me!"

—Isaiah 6:8, NIV

Not long ago I stumbled on a patch of rough
   ground and fell into a heap on the hard
   terrain.
Dazed and aching, I lay there afraid to move
   while a thousand thoughts raced through
   my mind.

*Did anyone see me? Will someone help me? Can I
    reach my smartphone? Did I break a hip? Will
    I have to have surgery?*
In a matter of seconds, life turned topsy-turvy.
O God, the wilderness of late life is pot-holed
    with disruptions.
I barely overcome one disruption before
    another appears in my path.
Some disruptions—like a health scare, a fall, a
    loss—shake me to the core.
Others are just irritating moments that inter-
    rupt my routine.
O God, I am learning that late life also has
    divine interruptions—the kind Jonah
    experienced when you sent him on an
    assignment to preach in Nineveh.
Like Jonah, I am often resistant to your call-
    ings that disrupt the routine of my life.
As I turn to go in the opposite direction, I
    conjure up a litany of excuses—
Not at my age. Not with my arthritis prob-
    lems. Not with weak eyes and hearing loss.

Maybe I could have done it when I was
    younger but not now. It is just too late.
Lord, your holy interruption is relentless. You
    chase me down again and again.
You interrupt my comfort with a constant
    nudging to follow your call in these late
    years.
In this wilderness of aging, give me the cour-
    age to say, "Here I am, Lord."

CULTIVATING HOPE

As a child, you probably learned the story of Jonah
and the big fish. God calls Jonah to preach in
Nineveh, a city with a wicked reputation. Jonah
does not want to go and sets sail on a ship headed
the opposite direction. God sends a violent storm,
and Jonah is heaved overboard. After spending
three days in the belly of the big fish, Jonah repents
and is spit out on dry land. Then God calls Jonah a
second time: "Go to the great city of Nineveh and
proclaim to it the message I give you" (Jon. 3:2,
NIV). This time Jonah answers the call.

Scripture is filled with stories of God interrupting someone's routine to fulfill God's holy purpose. Imagine what went through Moses' mind when God appeared to him in a burning bush and called him to lead God's people out of Egypt. Think how Mary and Joseph's lives were turned upside down when they discovered that Mary would give birth to Jesus. One thing is certain in the Christian life: Being faithful to God's call will bring divine interruptions, even in old age.

- If you think you have outgrown God's calling, think again. God is always calling you to do something, no matter your age or limitations. Even the frailest elderly person who spends their days in a wheelchair in a nursing home can be used by God to be an exceptional listener and a godly influence for young caregivers and aides.

  Look back at your life and pinpoint times when you tried to run from God's call. Why did you balk at what God asked you to do? What reasons did you give? What was the outcome? Think about times in the past when you have been obedient to God's call. What was the result? What did you learn from those experiences that can help you in this current season?

To help you discern what God is calling you to do in this season of late life, reflect on the following questions.

How are you currently experiencing the Spirit's persistent nudge?

What are you feeling prompted to do?

What is causing you to push back against a feeling or inner voice?

In what ways might you be trying to protect your own comfort?

Prayerfully consider your answers, then ask yourself if you are responding to God's call with stubborn rebellion or with faithful obedience.

Perhaps God is asking you to model a gracious acceptance of a caregiver's help when you have pridefully resisted it in the past. Maybe God wants you to embrace your fear of technology so you can participate in an online Bible study. It is possible that God is encouraging you to write your life stories as a testimony of your faith to younger family members.

Open yourself to the nudging of the Holy Spirit. Instead of becoming frustrated when your comfortable routine gets uprooted, learn to obediently accept divine interruption as an invitation to do something new. God still calls you to grow and serve others.

- Make a list of things you fear about pursuing a call from God. Are you afraid of what others will think? Are you fearful of being ridiculed or not appearing competent? Do you feel inadequate or too complacent? Are you allowing advanced age to limit your response to God's call? Remember that God will enable you beyond what you think are your limits. Invite the Spirit to speak to you today with this prayer:

Spirit of God, fall afresh on this aging body. I give to you all that I am—thinning hair, dimming eyes and ears, wrinkled hands, and arthritic joints. I want to be your faithful servant. Use my faltering body and my lifetime of experiences for your purposes. Amen.

Listen carefully. Accept the call by saying, *Here I am, Lord.*

Prayer

O God, do not be far from me;
O my God, make haste to help me!
—Psalm 71:12

Loneliness is my constant companion in old
 age.
Sometimes I cry out in the darkness but only
 hear the echo of my plea reverberating
 back to me.
O God, I know that you are not an aloof, dis-
 tant being. You have been my confidant
 through the years.

I have heard your voice in every season of my
life, yet now you seem silent.

I begin to doubt you and myself.

Perhaps my words are not eloquent enough.
Maybe you have grown weary of my
relentless requests.

Lord, I know you have granted me these long
years for a reason.

You have heard every prayer on my lips and
even those that went unvoiced.

I will take refuge in you, knowing your silence
has purpose.

Even as I pour out my worries, I will praise
you.

Though I express my complaints, I will bow in
awe of your power.

As I share the mundane details of my day, I
will remember that you know every gray
hair on my head.

O God, this wilderness is fertile ground for
my trust to grow.

Help me develop a deepening habit of prayer
so that when challenges come, I will turn
first to you.

As this old body wears down, let me be com-
forted by your constant presence even
when your voice seems silent.

Cultivating Hope

Older adults often worry about not being able to
adequately express their innermost thoughts to
God. You too may be concerned about fumbling
over your words, especially if asked to offer a public
prayer. Remember this important truth: God is not
impressed by lofty words. God yearns for authentic
hearts and people who want to grow in relationship
with God.

- Take a moment to honestly assess your current prayer life. How would you best describe
  it? Awkward? Mechanical? Inconsistent? Perhaps you have become too dependent on others praying for you. Or maybe you only think

about praying before a meal or when a crisis arises.

- Whatever your present circumstance, God wants to bring renewal to your prayer life. Take inspiration from Psalm 71, which, in some translations, is called the "Prayer in Time of Old Age." Read this passage and reflect on what the psalmist is saying about growing older with God.

Do not cast me off in the time of old
    age;
    do not forsake me when my
    strength is spent.
For my enemies speak concerning
    me,
    and those who watch for my life
    consult together.
They say, "Pursue and seize that
    person
    whom God has forsaken,
    for there is no one to deliver."

O God, do not be far from me;
    O my God, make haste to help
      me!
Let my accusers be put to shame and
      consumed;
    let those who seek to hurt me
    be covered with scorn and
      disgrace.
But I will hope continually,
    and will praise you yet more and
      more.
My mouth will tell of your righteous
      acts,
    of your deeds of salvation all day
      long,
    though their number is past my
      knowledge.
I will come praising the mighty
      deeds of the Lord God,
    I will praise your righteousness,
      yours alone.

O God, from my youth you have
  taught me,
  and I still proclaim your wondrous
  deeds.
So even to old age and gray hairs,
  O God, do not forsake me,
until I proclaim your might
  to all the generations to come.
Your power and your righteousness,
  O God,
  reach the high heavens.
  (Ps. 71:9-19)

In what ways can you relate to the thoughts and feelings of the psalmist? Do not be afraid to bring all your human emotions to God, from gratitude and overwhelming love to your greatest fears and deepest regrets. Prayer will help you deepen your relationship with God and better understand God's loving nature as you age.

■ Prayer exercises are another way to help you become more mindful of God's presence in your life. Embrace these fresh prayer experiences as you seek to strengthen your relationship with God.

- Place ten coins in your pocket. As you go through your daily routine, be mindful of unexpected blessings. With each blessing you experience, move a coin from one pocket to another and name the blessing aloud.

- Choose a special time and place to "meet with God." Of course, you can pray anywhere and at any time, but many older adults have discovered that designating a specific place and time strengthens their prayer life. One older saint faithfully met God on her piano bench early each evening. She played hymns and sang each verse as a prayerful way to connect with God. Create a space away from your usual easy chair and television so that you will be more intentional about distancing yourself from distractions and giving God your full attention.

— Set aside time for a daily walk, and choose a different prayer focus each day. One day, pray for every neighbor whose door you pass. On another day, give thanks for things you see in nature. Be creative and purposeful as you focus your attention on a particular topic.

Wisdom

The Lord *gives wisdom;*
from his mouth come knowledge
and understanding.
—Proverbs 2:6

On the back end of life, significant decisions
   must be made.
When should I quit driving? Who should I
   select as my power of attorney? Where
   should I go if I must move?
Navigating the journey of aging is complicated
   and consequential.

Over my span of years, I have made foolish
    choices at times.
Even now that I am older, the right answers to
    life's problems are sometimes elusive, and I
    struggle to choose wisely.
I have often heard that wisdom comes from
    age, but I've learned that saying isn't true.
Wisdom comes from God.
Here in the wilderness, I intermingle with
    other silver-haired elders who bicker and
    boast about petty things.
They have accumulated a lifetime of experi-
    ences and knowledge, but they are not
    godly wisdom-keepers.
True wisdom is steeped in a close relationship
    with you, Lord.
I cannot grow in wisdom apart from you.
It is your gift of clarity to me in a world of
    confusion and uncertainty.
O God, keep me from squandering the strug-
    gles and hardships of my long life.

Help me to glean your insight from those
   experiences.
Old age is a time of reaping wisdom, but it is
   also a time of sowing wisdom into the lives
   of others.
In a world that is often shallow and mis-
   guided, I long to share insight I have
   gained through years of walking with you,
   Lord.
Now give me wisdom to know how to share it.

CULTIVATING HOPE

It is often said that the world is starving for wisdom even though there is a barrage of information
online. With a click, you can know the number of
miles between Seattle and St. Louis. You can learn
the name of every US Vice President or the year
that penicillin was discovered. Never has the world
had so much information at its fingertips. Never-
theless, information alone is not wisdom.

   On the journey of aging, you have learned that
life's more difficult questions are seldom answered

with simple facts. These questions are nuanced and require wisdom and discernment. Though anyone can accumulate knowledge and facts, only God can give you true wisdom.

- When was the last time you asked God to increase your wisdom? Was there something you were trying to discern? If you knew God would help you make a wise decision about one thing at this stage of life, what would it be?

  Reflect on the following verse, and note what is required of you to grow in godly wisdom: "If any of you is lacking in wisdom, ask God, who gives to all generously and ungrudgingly, and it will be given you" (James 1:5). Notice that the first step to increased wisdom is to admit that you need it. Be humble enough to acknowledge that old age alone does not bring wisdom. Then ask God to give you the gift of wisdom.

- Once there was a minister who offered sage advice as he handed out Bibles to the third-graders in his congregation. He looked into their young eyes and said, "Grow old with your Bible." Wisdom is about taking the knowledge you collect from scripture and applying it to your daily life. It is more than an academic exercise to increase information. Wisdom is lived out in response to what you have learned from God's Word.

Spend time perusing your Bible for scripture verses that specifically mention wisdom. Start with the book of Proverbs. Highlight or underline every passage that speaks of wisdom. On another day, choose the book of Job, the Psalms, or Ecclesiastes. Think deeply about each passage as it relates to your life. Ask what God is saying to you for your late life. How might you put this wisdom into practice in your life?

- As you have aged, you have learned that things with eternal value come into clearer focus as things of the world fade away. Relationships become much more significant than possessions, awards, or power. With increased wisdom also comes the recognition that your earthly life is fleeting. Fixing your mind on these important truths will help you be both a wisdom-keeper and a godly witness. Reflect on this important question: If you were invited to offer three pieces of wisdom to younger generations, what would you tell them?

Finishing Well

I am confident of this, that the one who began a good work among you will bring it to completion by the day of Jesus Christ.

—Philippians 1:6

I don't worry about death; I worry about how I
   will die.
Will I linger in a state of frailty?
Will I be in a sterile hospital room, sur-
   rounded by beeping machines?
Will I die at home in my sleep, as I hope?

O Lord, at my age, thoughts of death and
dying are never far away.

The signs of aging are undeniable. There are
changes I cannot reverse.

Here in the wilderness, the finish line is
obscured by the dust and decay around me.

How long, O Lord? Send your Spirit! Bring
life and energy to these dry bones.

Open my eyes to a clear purpose that will pro-
pel me forward on this journey of aging.

Empower me to live fully when I am tempted
to hide in my room.

O God, you have given me a divine assignment: to grow in relationship with you, to
serve others in humility, and to glorify you
with every breath.

I have a unique story to share.

These late years are a holy privilege to become
the elder you want me to be.

On this homeward journey, stretch my faith
beyond my imagination.

Refocus my mind on gratitude and praise. You
　　have given me a mission to complete.
Help me to live by faith so I can live in hope.
Set my feet on the final path to glory.
The way of the cross will lead me home.

CULTIVATING HOPE

You do not need to be reminded that you are on
the home stretch. In this late season of life, it is a
sobering fact. Every day is another step closer to
the finish line. Yet no one knows the exact moment
when they will cross that line and enter into glory.

Perhaps you have already lived longer than you
ever expected. Or maybe you are hoping to make it
to a big milestone birthday or anniversary. Still, you
have concerns about how your late life will unfold.
You have watched close friends spend their last
years going in and out of the hospital and rehab.
You have known elders who struggled with chronic
disease or pain. Sometimes the burdens of old age
seem too heavy to bear. You say a silent prayer:
Please, Lord, do not let this be how my story ends.

- God does not guarantee you a carefree end-of-life story, but God does promise to be with you for every step of the journey. God also assures you of a divine purpose and the potential for profound growth and impact in your late years. Read these familiar verses from Psalm 92, and reflect on what the psalmist is saying about God's promise for late life:

The righteous flourish like the palm
      tree,
   and grow like a cedar in Lebanon.
They are planted in the house of the
      LORD;
   they flourish in the courts of our
      God.
In old age they still produce fruit;
   they are always green and full of
      sap. (Ps. 92:12-14)

Notice that it is the righteous who will flourish and produce fruit in old age and stay full of life. God's promise for new life is contingent upon your close walk with God now. God will help you flourish spiritually if you focus on relationship with God in your late years.

- Even if you have never set foot on a track or marathon course, you are running the race of life as set forth by your Creator. Ponder this passage from Philippians, then think deeply about how you are preparing to leave this world. Let the words of the apostle Paul inspire you to press on with endurance and grace:

> Forgetting what lies behind and
> straining forward to what lies ahead,
> I press on toward the goal for the
> prize of the heavenly call of God in
> Christ Jesus. (Phil. 3:13-14)

- The world desperately needs strong finishers to show others how to age faithfully. Do not waste a moment of your late life. Consider that your divine assignment in late life is threefold: to grow in relationship with God, to serve others with humility, and to glorify God in all that you do.

In what tangible ways will you complete that assignment today? What will you do to grow in your knowledge and understanding of who God is? How will you serve others in acts of humility? How will you share your testimony of God's faithfulness in your life with others?

- Think about someone you look to as a model for faithful aging. Who inspires you to serve others despite physical limitations? Maybe it is someone who has already passed on to glory, or perhaps it is someone in your current circle of friends. What characteristics does that person have that you want to emulate in late life? Be inspired! Practice those behaviors each day.

- Finally, think of your long life in terms of impact for God. You have been gifted with an extended opportunity to be an ambassador of God's love and grace. Name three people whose lives you will intentionally pour your life into from this day forward. Use your late years to be a difference-maker in their lives. Now is the time for fruitfulness in the wilderness. God is counting on you!

Standing on the Promises

My flesh and my heart may fail,
but God is the strength of my heart and my
portion forever.
—Psalm 73:26

There are mornings when it is almost impossible to pull my compression socks over my
swollen feet.
There are times when the chronic pain of
arthritis causes me to surrender the day to
my cushy chair.

Getting up from my seat is no longer the
effortless task it once was. Sometimes it
takes grit and courage.

Here in this wilderness of aging, the voice of
fear taunts me, saying that I have outlived
my purpose. That I am too old and slow.
That I am alone, and the journey ahead is
too strenuous.

In the Valley of Dry Bones, the Spirit stirs and
brings two words to my mind: *but God.*

Two words from scripture that change
everything.

Two words that bring hope from despair.

Two words that bring life from death.

What you promise, you will deliver, Lord.

When the wilderness experience seems insur-
mountable, you will make a way.

I can grow older with resilient hope because
you are always faithful to your promises.

It is hope that reminds me that you will never
leave me.

Hope says that you love me and that you
    created me in your image.
Hope pulls me up by my gnarled hands and
    shows me how to live with purpose until
    my final breath.
My hope is built on you, God Almighty.
My bones are yet alive!

CULTIVATING HOPE

In the wilderness of aging, you need more than cliché quotes about the importance of a positive attitude. You know the tough realities of growing older. You need authentic hope—the kind of hope that can conquer a growing list of fears running rampant in your mind.

It is not uncommon to experience an inner duel between hope and despair as you grow older. You desperately want to be hopeful, but fear and pain can be strong opponents. You struggle to rein in the negative thoughts that circle endlessly in your mind. How can you choose hope over despair? The answer is wrapped in a simple question: Who can you trust?

- Today read the lyrics of a favorite old hymn, "Standing on the Promises." Concentrate on the meaning of the lyrics. If you are familiar with the melody, sing it to yourself. Can you hear that strong, repeating bass line? Let this hymn or another sacred song of hope become a soundtrack for your life. Go to it daily. Sing the words over and over. Repeat the question: Who can I trust?

Standing on the promises of Christ
    my King,
Through eternal ages let his praises
    ring;
Glory in the highest, I will shout and
    sing,
Standing on the promises of God.

(Refrain)
Standing, standing,

Standing on the promises of God my
    Savior;
Standing, standing,
I'm standing on the promises of God.

Standing on the promises that can-
    not fail,
When the howling storms of doubt
    and fear assail,
By the living Word of God I shall
    prevail,
Standing on the promises of God.

(Refrain)

Standing on the promises of Christ
    the Lord,
Bound to him eternally by love's
    strong cord,
Overcoming daily with the Spirit's
    sword,
Standing on the promises of God.

(Refrain)

Standing on the promises I cannot
    fall,
List'ning ev'ry moment to the Spirit's
    call,
Resting in my Savior as my all in all,
Standing on the promises of God.

(Refrain)

Scripture is filled with the promises of God, from Genesis to Revelation. Open your Bible and search for passages about promises that God has made. Make an ongoing list. Fill your mind with God's assurance, and choose hope over despair.

- Spend time with five specific Bible passages in which the direction of the narrative totally changes with two short words: *but God.* After you read the verses on these pages, read them again from your own Bible to better understand the context. Reflect on each passage. Underline the phrase *but God* in each passage.

You intended to harm me, but God
intended it for good to accomplish
what is now being done, the saving
of many lives. (Gen. 50:20, NIV)

They are like sheep and are destined
    to die;
    death will be their shepherd
    (but the upright will prevail over
        them in the morning).
Their forms will decay in the grave,
    far from their princely mansions.
But God will redeem me from the
    realm of the dead;
    he will surely take me to himself.
        (Ps. 49:14-15, NIV)

All of us once lived among them
in the passions of our flesh, following the desires of flesh and senses,
and we were by nature children of
wrath, like everyone else. But God,
who is rich in mercy, out of the great

love with which he loved us even
when we were dead through our
trespasses, made us alive together
with Christ—by grace you have been
saved—and raised us up with him
and seated us with him in the heav-
enly places in Christ Jesus, so that in
the ages to come he might show the
immeasurable riches of his grace in
kindness toward us in Christ Jesus.
(Eph. 2:3-7)

Brothers and sisters, think of what
you were when you were called. Not
many of you were wise by human
standards; not many were influential;
not many were of noble birth. But
God chose the foolish things of the
world to shame the wise; God chose
the weak things of the world to shame
the strong. (1 Cor. 1:26-27, NIV)

When they had carried out everything that was written about him,
they took him down from the tree
and laid him in a tomb. But God
raised him from the dead. (Acts
13:29-30)

Today invite the Spirit to breathe new
life into your weary bones. Because of God's
faithfulness and grace, you can live with
unshakable hope, no matter your age or circumstances. Complete each sentence with
one of God's promises. Rise up and live!

I feel as if I have outlived my purpose, but
God _____.

It seems no one notices me anymore, but
God _____.

I feel vulnerable and exposed in this aging
body, but God _____.

I would like to hide out in my room, but
God _____.

The world tells me that aging is my enemy, but God _____.

I feel incapable of learning new things, but God _____.

I feel I am too old to make changes, but God _____.